Landmark
insights.
Book 1

Live a Life You Love

Landmark®

Published by
Landmark Worldwide
353 Sacramento St., Ste. 200
San Francisco, CA 94111

ISBN-13: 978-0615876573
ISBN-10: 0615876579

Printed in the United States of America
First Edition

This book points out what is possible if we step outside of what we know, and recognize and embrace our capacity to bring forth an entirely new possibility for living—not because it is better, but simply because that is what human beings can do.

The Lens Through Which We See—
Fixed or Open to Invention?

"I used to wonder if children who wore glasses saw better or only different worlds…. Whatever reality may be, it will be shaped by the lens through which we see it. When we are born we are handed multiple lenses: genetic inheritance, gender, a specific culture and the variables of our family environment, all of which constitute our sense of reality. Looking back later, we see that we have perhaps lived less from our true nature than from the vision of reality ordained by the lenses we used."[1]

The good news is that our actions are not correlated to some reality ordained by those lenses, but rather to how the world "occurs" to us. With the unsettling of old realities, stepping to one side and another, we become interested in what might be, what we can imagine. "Reality" is a phenomenon that arises in language. Language is both the ultimate reality and the medium through which reality is brought forth—there is no reality "per se," no fixed reality. There's only how we see it, how we say it is—it's interpretation all the way down. It's language—what we say (with and about others, ourselves, and the world at large) that constitutes *who we are*. Getting that at the most fundamental level alters the very nature of what's possible—not merely in the way we think about ourselves, but in the actual experience and expression of *who we are*. Language is inseparable from *who we are*, and what gives us access to our true nature—to the full panoply of being human.

Choice: The Word that Allows for "Yes"

It's the word that allows yes and the word that makes no possible.
It's the word that puts the free in freedom and takes obligation out of the mix.
It's the word upon which adventure, exhilaration, and authenticity depend.
It's the word that the cocoon whispers to the caterpillar.[2]

We tell ourselves sometimes that living a transformed life isn't that important, that it's enough just to get by. We get wrapped up in our own concerns, particular points of view, or positions, and the idea of getting ourselves to a place where things can be great seems too big an undertaking. If somebody had a magic powder to come and sprinkle on us and just through that we'd be transformed, we might say, "No, thanks–I don't want any! Let me stay just as I am." It takes courage to live in a transformed way–to wrestle with our resistances, to give up mediocrity, to live consistent with what we know is possible in being human. It's always and only a matter of our choosing.

Right/Wrong or an Honored Place in the Dialogue

"…In virtually every human society, 'he hit me first' or 'he started it' provides an acceptable rationale for what comes next. It's thought that a punch thrown second is legally and morally different than a punch thrown first. The problem with the principle of even-numberedness is that people count differently. People think of their own actions as the consequences of what came before, they think of other people's actions as the causes of what came later, and that their reasons and pains are more palpable, more obvious and real, than that of others."[3]

These are positions and ideas we all "wind up" playing out. When we "are" right, embedded in that truth is an equal truth that someone else is *wrong*–it's not a matter of accuracy, it's a matter of *being*. We can't *be* happy, vital, and loving while we're *being* right, making someone wrong, or justifying our positions–one displaces the other. The "rightness" of our positions pretty much precludes us from hearing and seeing other points of view.

We have a choice about what's at play. When we elect to transform ways we *wound up being*, we move to a place of freedom, a place of possibility. Our points of view and positions can then move from fixed to malleable, from closed to open–where each person has an honored place in the dialogue.

Relationships: *Being* Satisfied

"When relationships are driven by complaint or by keeping track of who did what, or the need to be right, to control, the wonderful world of human possibilities ceases to reverberate through them."[4] Possibilities between people require a space in which to create, and when that space isn't there, most likely it's because we're holding on to something incomplete from the past. Completing things comes down to a matter of getting beyond the "yeah buts," the "how 'bouts," the "but ifs," past our old assumptions about "the way things have been."

When we experience things as being complete, it's a state change, from being a character in a story to being the space in which the stories occurs—to being the author, as it were. And because relationships exist in language (instead of, for example, a set of feelings or accumulation of experiences), there's a malleability, a plasticity, a can-be moved-around-ness about them. When we shift the locus of our dissatisfaction and complaints from something that exists "out there," to something that's located "in" what we are saying (language), what's possible shifts.

Being satisfied is not a feeling later labeled with the word "satisfaction," rather it is a commitment, a stand we're taking for that possibility. It's a transformation—a contextual shift from being organized around "getting satisfied" to an experience of "being satisfied"—that alters the very nature of what's possible.

"Why isn't it O.K. for us to have different mirages?"

When Old Frames Stop Defining Who We Are

Roman chariots and carts were built to be the width of two horses. Roads throughout the Roman Empire were built to be the same width. Coaches, trains, and cars followed, all the same width. *Fast forward to space travel*–the solid fuel rocket engines, in order to be transported by rail, had to be designed the same width...A major design feature of *our most advanced transportation system* was set more than 2,000 years ago by the width of two horses. Knowledge that's handed down, inherited like this, is in one sense "everybody else's," yet we often (for better or worse), end up living within its parameters.

Our contexts–how we hold things–sets the values, limitations, and direction of our daily lives. They impose on the external world our version of reality. It can take a long time to shift our contexts–not because it takes a long time to bring about change, but because we go about it at the level of "content." In dealing with the content, we are extending the existing world rather than creating a new possibility in the world. When we function at a level of context instead of content, old frames stop defining who we are. It's not that we escape them–it is rather that we escape thinking automatically, reflexively. Nothing is more exciting than to see the world in a new way, because we don't see one new thing–we see everything in a new way.

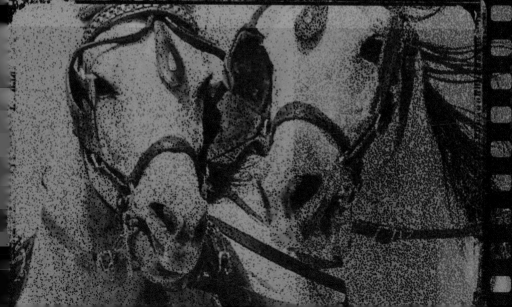

The Stone Must Gravitate and
Tiger Must Pounce. Only Human Beings...

The stone and the tiger have no choice of life. The stone must gravitate and tiger must pounce. Only human beings are faced with the mind-boggling responsibility of having to choose, at each and every moment of their lives, what to do and what to be. It is both a necessity and an invitation.[5]

Transformation is about coming to grips with what it means to be human. It prompts us toward risk–a risk inseparable from living–that carries with it a wisdom and a knowing that that choice is ours. It's from there that the full range available to us in being human can be explored and lived.

Power and Freedom Where Fear Used to Be

"Bob Slocum, a hero in a Joseph Heller novel, is a middling executive at an unnamed company who's driven nearly mad thinking that decisions might be made behind his back that could ruin his career and his life. He's not alone in these thoughts. Slocum says, 'In the office there are five people of whom I am afraid. Each of these five people is afraid of four people (excluding overlaps), for a total of 20, and each of those people is afraid of six people, making a total of 120 people who are feared by at least one person.' The company is a pyramid of potential panic, ready to topple when someone whispers, 'Jig's up.'"[6]

Perhaps even more than sadness or anger, we find it difficult to deal with fear. Fear often keeps us from doing what we're capable of–from experiencing and expressing the full range of what's possible in being human. This is not so much a function of the fear being operative, but rather of the automatic way we pull in our past experience. Old circumstances have the power, not us.

Completing a past fear includes recognizing that we would survive if the past repeated itself. There's a big difference between being realistic about what happened once, and thinking things will go that way again. We have the freedom to choose our relationship to *whatever-it-was* back then, and that's the beginning of building power. It takes enormous courage to try out new ways of being in the space where fear used to be.

Past/Present vs. Future/Present: Reversing the Flow

Possibility is an element of temporality, of time. We are localized in the present, but our overlay—our relationship to the present—is never just the present itself, it's either the past/present or the present/future. Of the two, the pull invariably is for the past/present—we can see its pull everywhere, especially when we have a good or bad experience.

We locate the memories of those experiences and the decisions we made about them out in front of us, in other words, in our future. Our future then becomes shaped and filtered through those decisions, limiting what's even seen or imagined as possible.

Starting from possibility reverses the flow—it becomes a future/present pull, which changes the game entirely. Even at its earliest stages, possibility leaves us with power and freedom. Altering the temporality of things is not just a matter of time—it's a matter of the quality of our lives.

Present/Past

Happiness Is an Inside Job

Some of us think happiness is dependent on things outside of ourselves—we'll be happy when… or happy because… or happy if…. Others think of happiness as a rare and fleeting thing, or are dubious from the start that it's even possible, kind of like there's an underlying position or commitment of "I'm not happy." If that's true about you, it is a pretty useful thing to know.

Being happy can't have some "thing" in mind because it is not some "thing" in the foreground; it's a background stand that creates the possibility of what's in the foreground. "I am happy," is a matter of saying—a sacred saying, a saying that has no ground underneath it, but becomes the ground. No rationale, no evidence. Being happy exists as a possibility—it's an inside job. If we can say, "I am happy," and it's true because we said so, that's power, instantaneous, and timeless. And that's the ultimate act of creativity.

Being Authentic—a Matter of Courage

When we compromise, even in the tiniest of matters, it's easier for those compromises to become more and more commonplace. Over time, bit by bit, this erodes our sense of self. While one drop of red paint in a can of white may turn the paint only the palest shade of pink—perhaps barely noticeable—no matter what we say about it, the paint is no longer what it was. Similarly, when the wholeness and completeness of who we are is jeopardized in some way, albeit imperceptible at first, our sense of ourselves gets obscured, making it harder to return to who we are. When that begins, there's really no starting point to become ourselves—it's all flailing around.

The possibility of fully being ourselves occurs in proportion to our being authentic. Living with a pretense, or being afraid that some aspect of ourselves might be found out, precludes any real freedom. There is no template to follow, no zeitgeist to read, no known path to success. It's a matter of courage—it gets made up as we go along, and it is this shift that makes available to us the full possibility of being human.

Possibility—It Flies on Mighty Wings

"When we don't pay heed to the dance with uncertainty–when we limit the ambiguity, the floundering about, the experimentation–we deprive ourselves of the raw stuff of being fully alive."[7]

There is one kind of certainty that has to do with the predictable, inevitable, figure-out-able, having evidence. There's another that's brought forth not of circumstance and not of mind, not of prediction–but from taking a stand. This kind of certainty is based on questions rather than answers, on openness rather than resoluteness–there's no dogma, no rules, no need for justification or explanation. This second kind of certainty exists in the realm of risk, of having something at stake. It's that realm of risk and that kind of certainty where possibility comes alive and flourishes.

Whatever possibility is, it's born from a continuous "I don't know." This is why I value that little phrase so highly. It's small, but it flies on mighty wings. It expands our lives to include the spaces within us, as well as those outer expanses.[8]

In stepping outside of what we know, it's possible to bring forth an entirely new possibility for living not because it's better, but simply because it's what human beings can do.

...that little phrase,

I DON'T KNOW

Überfail, Massive Fail, Epic Fail—Who's to Say?

"At one time, *fail* was simply a verb that denoted being unsuccessful or falling short of expectations. Since then phrases like überfail, massive fail, or, most popular of all, epic fail have made occasional forays into nounhood."[9] We take the notion of failure for granted. We don't really even think about it. When we make up our mind to do something a particular way, and don't succeed, we think of it like it's a failure in ourselves, a "failure in *being*" vs. "*it* failed."

If we identify ourselves with achievement and accomplishment and success, it can be difficult to tolerate anything that's inconsistent with that, leaving us no powerful way to *be*. When we don't separate out what we were out to accomplish from our attitudes and feelings about it not turning out (i.e., the disparity between what happened and what the possibility was), that disparity is often interpreted as a "failure in being." This adds even more mass to the experience and reduces being able "to be" at all (i.e., überfail, epic fail, etc).

If we can effectively *be* with "that it didn't work," there's nothing but power there—instead of having it imply a *failure in being,* what's there to be addressed is the possibility of *inventing being.* The "being" part of being human is where the infinite possibility of living actually lies—where we are able to connect dots we never even knew were dots, go in directions we couldn't previously have considered, stand where we're able to see clearly for ourselves.

The Difference Between 99% and 100% Is Everything

If in the making of a computer chip or a bicycle wheel some small part were left out, neither would be able to function as intended. Any disruption in the integrity of something's design, however small, impacts its workability and function. When something is whole and complete, it is not good per se, it just works.

The same holds true in being human. When the wholeness and completeness of who we are is jeopardized in some way, however small, that begins to alter our life, even if at first it's imperceptible. We might experience a sense of discomfort; spend time defending, explaining, or pointing fingers; find ourselves tolerating a level of unworkability that we might not normally put up with. And because this happens in small increments, we don't fully get the kind of impact it has on things not working in our lives.

A baseline that was once at 100% now is at 99 or 98 or 70%. But it's that difference between 99 and 100% that's everything–it's in that 1% that the quality of our life gets altered. Our sense of ourselves becomes more and more obscured, making it harder and harder over time to return to who we are. In being true to ourselves, being authentic, we tip the scales. Integrity and living a life of power and effectiveness are inseparable.

Unwiring the Hardwiring—
Being Fully Ourselves

It often seems like our past experience is calling the shots. Here's how it works: When things don't go well, we put that past experience into our "future," as something we're afraid might happen again, and something we want to make sure doesn't. Or if things go well, we store that past experience in the future, too. So essentially, we take our experiences, which are behind us, and put our decisions about them–how we feel and think about them–in front of us. In doing so, we lock ourselves into relating to the past as if it were going to happen again in the future. That's the wiring.

Trying to resist or avoid the enormous influence of the past keeps us foolishly focused on it. Yet we're reluctant to leave it behind, reluctant to transform the hold it has on our present-time lives. Not doing so, however, results in a "now" that's shaped by and littered with the stuff of the past.

In recognizing that the "wiring" is calling the shots instead of us, we're left with nothing–nothing like a "clearing," one in which we can be fully ourselves. It is from nothing that a "created future" can come into the picture. If we're going to create a future–in our relationships, in our work, in our lives–it's a matter of saying so. It doesn't rest on anything–it rests on nothing and that's the foundation for possibility. In creating possibility, we get to know what's possible in being human.

A fundamental principle of Landmark's work is that people and the communities and organizations with which they are engaged have the possibility of not only success, but also fulfillment and greatness. It is to this possibility that Landmark and its work are committed.

www.landmarkworldwide.com

Endnotes

1. James Hollis, *The Middle Passage* (Inner City Books, 1993).

2. Adapted from Tom Robbins, *Still Life with Woodpecker* (Bantam Dell, 1980).

3. Adapted from Daniel Gilbert, "He Who Cast the First Stone Probably Didn't," *The New York Times*, 24 July 2006.

4. Adapted from Adrienne Rich, *Arts of the Possible* (W.W. Norton, 2002).

5. Jose Ortega y Gasset

6. Thomas A. Stewart, *Seeing Things*, Harvard Business Review (February 2008).

7. Denise Shekerjian, *Uncommon Genius* (Penguin Books, 1990).

8. Adapted from Wislawa Szymborska, *Poems New and Collected 1957-1997* (Harcourt, 1998).

9. Adapted from Ben Zimmer, "How Fail Went From Verb to Interjection," *The New York Times*, 9 August 2009.

6362479R10021

Made in the USA
San Bernardino, CA
07 December 2013